The Cross

'Deeply biblical, yet wonderfully accessible. This incredible thirty-day devotional looks at the very heart of the gospel, the cross, in a way that will have a profound impact on every Christian. A must-read.'
Gavin Calver, CEO, Evangelical Alliance

'Since the cross is central to God's grace-filled intervention in his creation, it is natural that it should lie at the heart of a spiritual centre of gravity. This series of studies, mined from many years of Keswick teaching, is a lovely means of keeping our focus on the cross, and I can see it doing the world of good to everyone who uses it.'
Mark Meynell, Director (Europe & Caribbean), Langham Preaching, Langham Partnership and author of Cross-Examined

30-DAY DEVOTIONAL

The Cross

Edited by Elizabeth McQuoid

INTER-VARSITY PRESS
36 Causton Street, London SW1P 4ST, England
Email: ivp@ivpbooks.com
Website: www.ivpbooks.com

First published 2021

British Library Cataloguing-in-Publication Data
A catalogue record for this book is available from the British Library.

ISBN: 978–1–78974–191–9
eBook ISBN: 978–1–78974–192–6

Set in Avenir 11/15pt
Typeset in Great Britain by CRB Associates, Potterhanworth, Lincolnshire
Printed in Great Britain by Ashford Colour Press Ltd, Gosport, Hampshire

Produced on paper from sustainable forests

Inter-Varsity Press publishes Christian books that are true to the Bible and that communicate the gospel, develop discipleship and strengthen the church for its mission in the world.

IVP originated within the Inter-Varsity Fellowship, now the Universities and Colleges Christian Fellowship, a student movement connecting Christian Unions in universities and colleges throughout Great Britain, and a member movement of the International Fellowship of Evangelical Students. Website: www.uccf.org.uk. That historic association is maintained, and all senior IVP staff and committee members subscribe to the UCCF Basis of Faith.

Contributors

Isaiah 53
Charles Price

Charles was Principal of Capernwray Bible School before becoming Senior Pastor of the People's Church, Toronto, in 2001. He is now the church's pastor-at-large. His sermons can be heard on his weekly television programme, *Living Truth*, which is broadcast around the world.

Matthew 27
Don Carson

Don is Research Professor of New Testament at Trinity Evangelical Divinity School in Deerfield, Illinois. He has written more than fifty books, serves on several boards and is a guest lecturer in academic and church settings around the world. Along with Tim Keller, he founded The Gospel Coalition.

John 19
Bruce Milne

Until 2001 Bruce was the pastor of First Baptist Church in Vancouver, Canada. Previously he taught at Spurgeon's

College. He is the author of *Know the Truth*, *Dynamic Diversity* and, in the Bible Speaks Today series, *The Message of John*.

Romans 8:30
Simon Manchester

Simon was for thirty years Senior Minister at St Thomas' Anglican Church, North Sydney, Australia. He studied at Moore Theological College in the Diocese of Sydney and was a curate at St Helen's Bishopsgate, London. Now retired, he spends his time writing and speaking around the world.

1 Corinthians 1:17 – 2:5
Vaughan Roberts

Vaughan has been Rector of St Ebbe's Church, Oxford, since 1998. He is Director of Proclamation Trust, an organization which encourages and equips Bible teachers. He is the author of many books, including *God's Big Picture*, *True Spirituality* and *Battles Christians Face*.

Philippians 2:1–18
Angus MacLeay

Angus is Rector of St Nicholas Church in Sevenoaks, Kent. Before moving there, he worked as a curate at Holy Trinity Platt and was Vicar of Houghton with Kingmoor in Carlisle.

Colossians 1:20
Liam Goligher
Liam has served as a pastor in Ireland, Canada, London and in his native Scotland. Since 2011 he has been Senior Minister at Tenth Presbyterian Church in Philadelphia, USA.

Colossians 1:21–23
Alasdair Paine
Alasdair is the vicar of The Round Church at St Andrew the Great, Cambridge, and a trustee of Keswick Ministries. He previously worked at St Leonard's Exeter and Christ Church Westbourne, Bournemouth.

Titus 2:11–14
Alistair Begg
Alistair has been Senior Pastor at Parkside Church, Ohio, since 1983. He has written a number of books including *Pray Big* and the Food for the Journey volume *Ruth*. He is also the voice behind the daily radio broadcast *Truth for Life*.

Hebrews 10:8–18
Alec Motyer
Alec was Vice Principal of Clifton Theological College and Vicar of St Luke's, Hampstead, before becoming

Principal of Trinity College, Bristol. He was much loved on both sides of the Atlantic as a Bible expositor and a prolific author.

1 John 3:1–10
Jeremy McQuoid

Jeremy is Teaching Pastor of Deeside Christian Fellowship Church, Aberdeen, and Chair of Keswick Ministries. He is a trustee of Pathways, an initiative to encourage more men and women into full-time gospel work in Scotland, and co-author of *The Amazing Cross* and several daily devotional guides.

Preface

What is the collective name for a group of preachers? A troop, a gaggle, a chatter, a pod . . . ? I'm not sure! But in this Food for the Journey series we have gathered an excellent group of Bible teachers to help us unpack the Scriptures and understand some of the core issues every Christian needs to know.

Each book is based on a particular theme and contains excerpts from messages given by much-loved Keswick Convention speakers, past and present. Where necessary, the language has been updated but, on the whole, this is what you would have heard had you been listening in the tent on Skiddaw Street. A wide, though not exhaustive, selection of Bible passages explore the key theme, and each day of the devotional ends with a fresh section designed to help you apply God's Word to your own life and situation.

Whether you are a Convention regular or have never been to Keswick, this Food for the Journey series is a unique opportunity to study the Scriptures and a particular topic with a range of gifted Bible teachers by your side. Each book is designed to fit in your jacket pocket or handbag, so you can read it anywhere – over the breakfast table, on the commute into work or college, while you are waiting in your car, over your lunch break or in bed at night. Wherever life's journey takes you, time in God's Word is vital nourishment for your spiritual journey.

Our prayer is that these devotionals become your daily feast, a nourishing opportunity to meet with God through his Word. Read, meditate, apply and pray through the Scriptures given for each day, and allow God's truths to take root and transform your life.

If these devotionals whet your appetite for more, there is a 'For further study' section at the end of each book. You can also visit our website www.keswickministries.org to find the full range of books, study guides, CDs, DVDs and mp3s available.

Let the word of Christ dwell in you richly.
(Colossians 3:16, ESV)

Introduction
Discovering treasure

When my boys were little, they loved treasure hunts. They would draw maps, follow the clues, and when they found the treasure, would shriek with delight, 'X marks the spot.'

For Christians, 'X' truly does mark the spot. The cross of Christ, though a place of torture and inexpressible agony, is also a place of unfathomable treasure. It is the end of our searching – the place where we find forgiveness and healing, where we meet with God, where we see the full extent of his love for us, where we learn that victorious living actually looks a lot like dying.

On that first Good Friday many would have seen the darkened sky and Jesus' lifeless body, and concluded that God had been defeated. But, from eternity's perspective, Jesus was never more powerful and glorious. On the cross he was conquering sin, Satan and death once and for all. He was displaying God's indisputable sovereignty, good-ness and love to every generation and culture. The cross was not a tragic accident, or the outcome of cruel men getting the upper hand. It was the culmination of God's salvation plan where the sin of the world met the full force of his holiness. Jesus took my place, dying the death I deserved. He paid the penalty for sin and satisfied God's wrath, making a relationship with him possible.

At the cross we see that not only is God *for* us, he is *with* us. Jesus became one of us – sharing the muck, madness and mundanity of our lives. His death conclusively refutes the charge that God is distant and dismissive of our suffering. The crown of thorns, the betrayal of friends, the taunts of his enemies, the nails driven through his hands and feet reveal a God who understands our pain and stands with us in it.

Jesus' death on the cross was a once-in-a-lifetime event, but our coming to the cross cannot be. When we became Christians, our sins – past, present and future – were forgiven. We became children of God, welcomed into his family, sharing the status and privileges of Jesus. However, we still sin and need to keep coming back to the cross for daily cleansing. As Christ's followers, we are to feel the crossbeam chafe against our lives and priorities. Jesus said, 'Whoever wants to be my disciple must deny themselves and take up their cross daily and follow me' (Luke 9:23). When Jesus took up his cross, he was submitting himself wholly to his Father's will, and that's what it means for us too. It is a daily surrender of ourselves and our agenda to God. Carrying our cross will transform every-thing – our singleness, marriage, parenting, work and retirement. It has an impact on how we spend our money, serve in church, and on the leisure interests we pursue.

This devotional brings together a selection of Bible pas-sages about the cross to help us appreciate its power and what it means for our daily lives. Prophecies, eyewitness accounts, letters to churches and individuals, all underline that we can never sideline the message of the cross, we can never outgrow it, and we can't sugar-coat it to make it more palatable for secular ears. The cross is not just a symbol of Christianity, it stands at its core. There can be no 'good news' without it.

It is indeed true: 'X marks the spot.'

Isaiah

Isaiah had the unenviable task of warning the people of Judah that continued sin would result in judgement at the hands of the Babylonians. They would be carried off into exile, the city of Jerusalem would be destroyed, and restoration would only begin when God's servant, King Cyrus of Persia, allowed the Jews to return home. The prophet also spoke about a servant of God greater than Cyrus. He prophesied about a Messiah, descended from David, who would rule righteously, and through whose suffering complete salvation would be achieved. Written about 700 years in advance, chapter 53 points forward with breathtaking clarity to Jesus' death on the cross for our sins.

Day 1

Read Isaiah 53
Key verses: Isaiah 53:4, 10

....

Surely he took up our pain
and bore our suffering,
yet we considered him punished by God,
stricken by him, and afflicted.

¹⁰Yet it was the Lᴏʀᴅ's will to crush him and cause
him to suffer,
and though the Lᴏʀᴅ makes his life an offering
for sin,
he will see his offspring and prolong his days,
and the will of the Lᴏʀᴅ will prosper in his hand.

For whom did Jesus die?

You might answer, 'Jesus died for the world,' or 'Jesus died for sinners,' or you may personalize it and say, 'Jesus died for me.' All those statements contain truth, because we are the beneficiaries of his death, but we are not the primary reason why Jesus died and why the cross was necessary. In the first instance, Jesus died for his Father. Verses 4 and 10 indicate it was God who required the cross.

We would prefer a simpler remedy for sin. We would rather just say 'sorry' for our sin, and have God forgive us. But that is not enough, because the problem with sin is not just that it messes with our lives, but that it violates God's righteousness and provokes his wrath. It is that which is to be addressed. What lies behind the cross is not in the first instance the love of God, although love is his very nature, but his wrath. The brutality of the cross is an expression of God's anger at sin.

God put Jesus Christ forward to address and satisfy his wrath. A good word to describe this is 'propitiation', which means to turn away wrath by satisfying its demands and requirements. Romans 3:24–25 explains that we are 'justified by his grace as a gift, through the redemption that is in Christ Jesus, whom God put forward as a propitiation by his blood, to be received by faith' (ESV), and 1 John 2:2 says, 'He is the propitiation for our sins, and not for ours only but also for the sins of the whole world' (ESV).

We don't like the idea that God's anger needs to be addressed. But the Bible teaches that Jesus was not just stricken by evil men, but stricken by God (verse 4). Verses 6 and 10 say, 'The LORD has laid on him the iniquity of us all . . . Yet it was the LORD's will to crush him . . . the LORD makes his life an offering for sin.' The wrath of God was poured out on Christ as our substitute, standing in our place that we might be forgiven.

I believe a word that forcefully captures the essence of Jesus' work of propitiation is the word exhausted. Jesus exhausted the wrath of God. It was not merely deflected and prevented from reaching us; it was exhausted. Jesus bore the full, unmitigated brunt of it. God's wrath against sin was unleashed in all its fury on His beloved Son. He held nothing back.
(Jerry Bridges, *The Gospel for Real Life*, NavPress, 2002, p. 56)

Heavenly Father, thank you that you held nothing back. You poured out all of your wrath at my sin on your Son so that I would never experience it. Lord Jesus, thank you that you stood in my place willingly. Help me grow to hate sin as much as you do. Give me strength to tackle sins which have become habitual, and avoid temptations. May my obedience bring you pleasure today. Amen.

Day 2

Read Isaiah 53
Key verse: Isaiah 53:11

••

After he has suffered,
he will see the light of life and be satisfied;
by his knowledge my righteous servant will justify
many,
and he will bear their iniquities.

What did Jesus accomplish on the cross? Scripture says he 'justified' us. What does that mean? It is more than saying we are forgiven.

Justified is a legal term meaning that justice has been served and satisfied. When Britain had capital punishment, in Scotland if a man was hanged, a notice was posted outside the prison announcing the hanging. It had certain required legal language and would say, 'On such-and-such a date, at Market Cross, so-and-so [naming the prisoner] was justified.' What did it mean? Did it mean the prisoner had been forgiven? No, it meant justice had been satisfied, the case had been closed and could never be resurrected in a court of law again.

Justification is much deeper than forgiveness. It means the case against us is over, it has been legally satisfied. It is finished.

Of course it is true that the mercy and love of God lie behind the cross, but if God were to forgive us on the basis of mercy alone, we might be forgiven, but we would not be justified. We are justified on the basis that Jesus satisfied the justice of God. We may wonder as we confess the same sin that we have confessed so many times before if we've come to the point of exhausting God's mercy. But we appeal not to his mercy, but to his justice! When we appeal to his justice, God is legally and morally obligated to forgive. 'He is faithful and *just* to forgive us our sins and to cleanse us from all unrighteousness' (1 John 1:9, ESV, emphasis added).

When we come in repentance and say, 'I have failed again. Father, would you forgive me?', he looks at the cross, and our sin is paid for. Don't let past sins condemn you any more. Because Christ has absorbed the justice of God, the case against you is over.

As we come to Christ . . . empty-handed, claiming no merit of our own, but clinging by faith to His blood and righteousness, we are justified. We pass immediately from a state of condemnation and spiritual death to a state of pardon, acceptance, and the sure hope of eternal life. Our sins are blotted out, and we are 'clothed' with the righteousness of Jesus Christ. In our standing before God, we will never be more righteous, even in heaven, than we were the day we trusted Christ, or we are now.

(Jerry Bridges, *The Gospel for Real Life*, NavPress, 2002, p. 107)

We are justified. The penalty for our sin has been paid, and the case against us is closed. Of course, in our daily lives we still sin and fall short of the perfect righteous-ness God requires. But don't give up. Keep on coming to God for forgiveness. The Puritans called this 'renewing our repentance' – asking God to take the forgiveness he has already granted through Christ's death and apply it to our sins today. And keep on pursuing holiness, asking for Holy Spirit power to become what we are – righteous in God's sight.

Day 3

Read Isaiah 53
Key verse: Isaiah 53:9

....

He was assigned a grave with the wicked,
and with the rich in his death,
though he had done no violence,
nor was any deceit in his mouth.

Are you plagued with guilt for past sin?

We need to know that not only have we been justified, but our sin has been buried. At Calvary Jesus bore our sin, he satisfied the wrath of God, and he legally removed our guilt so that we are justified. And having died, he was buried. Because of our union with Christ, not only have we died with him; we – including our sin – are buried with him too (Romans 6:4).

Historically, Jesus should not have been buried, because in Jerusalem the bodies of criminals were thrown into a deep narrow gorge on the south side of the city, which is known as the Valley of Gehenna. In Jesus' day it was known as the rubbish dump of Jerusalem, where a fire burned continually. But Jesus was not placed there, because Joseph of Arimathea, a member of the Sanhedrin, approached Pilate to ask for the body of Jesus (John 19:38). With Pilate's permission, Joseph took Jesus' body away, buried him in his own tomb, and this remarkable prophecy in Isaiah 53:9 was fulfilled.

There is a finality to burial. The time between death and burial is usually a difficult period for loved ones. But once burial has taken place, it is final. In being 'buried with Christ', we don't need to feel guilt over our confessed sins because they have been fully and finally buried with Christ. 'Therefore, there is now no condemnation for those who are in Christ Jesus' (Romans 8:1).

So whenever we feel condemned, we can be sure it is not God speaking to us. The devil is the one who accuses us before God day and night (Revelation 12:10). There are two who speak to us about our sins: the devil and the Holy Spirit. The devil condemns but the Holy Spirit convicts. Here is the difference: condemnation is like a wet blanket that sits on us and we can't get out from under it; conviction makes us aware of our sin, but at the same time the Holy Spirit points us to the cross and offers cleansing and forgiveness.

Whose voice are you listening to?

When the devil whispers to us about our sin, he breathes hopelessness and despair. 'Your friends would be horrified if they knew what you had done.' 'With your track record, you can't possibly serve God.' 'You'll never escape this cycle of sin.' Don't listen to the devil's condemnation, but remind him your sin has been buried.

In contrast, when the Holy Spirit speaks, we are cut to the heart, realizing how much our sin grieves God and how much it cost the Lord Jesus. But this conviction comes with the offer of forgiveness, hope and renewal. It comes with the comfort that there is 'no condemnation for those who are in Christ'. Today listen for the Spirit's voice, repent when he highlights your sin, and rely on his strength to live out your new life 'in Christ'.

Day 4

Read Isaiah 53
Key verse: Isaiah 53:12

....

Therefore I will give him a portion among the great,
and he will divide the spoils with the strong,
because he poured out his life unto death,
and was numbered with the transgressors.
For he bore the sin of many,
and made intercession for the transgressors.

What is a transgressor? It is a law-breaker, and everyone has broken God's law (1 John 3:4; Romans 3:23).

At the cross Jesus was 'numbered among the transgressors'. He was identified as one of us. He became a sinner in his standing before the Father. He who knew no sin was made to be sin for us (2 Corinthians 5:21). He did this so that he might intercede for transgressors, speak to God on our behalf. So he says to the Father, 'Charles Price has sinned again. He has confessed. I'm on his side, I am his defender and advocate. On the grounds of my own death, he is forgiven; he is justified.'

This is the language of substitution. Christ was made sin and stood in my place, I am made righteous and stand in his place. His sin was not about him, but it was about me; and my righteousness is not about me, but it's about him. He received our infirmities, our sorrows, our transgressions, iniquities and punishment. And we received his peace, healing and righteousness (verses 4–5).

It is important to grasp this teaching on substitution. First, it reminds us that our godliness has nothing to do with how well we perform, but everything to do with the sufficiency of what Jesus did on the cross. Second, it challenges us about doubting our forgiveness. It is not being humble to doubt your forgiveness, because you are actually doubting Jesus. Of course we don't deserve forgiveness, but when we doubt that we are clean before God, we doubt the effectiveness of the cross. It says in 1 John 4:17, 'This is how love is made complete among us so that we will have confidence on the day of judgment.'

On that final day we are going to stand before God with confidence – not self-confidence, pride or arrogance, but in utter humility, confident that Jesus Christ is enough.

Are you doubting whether God can really forgive your sins? Are you measuring yourself by your own goodness? Will you trust that Jesus' death in your place is sufficient – sufficient to make you clean before God now, sufficient one day to stand before him, blameless and approved, sufficient for him to be as delighted with you as he is with Christ?

> In Christianity, the moment we believe, God imputes Christ's perfect performance to us as if it were our own, and adopts us into His family. In other words, God can say to us just as He once said to Christ, 'You are My Son, whom I love; with you I am well pleased.'
> (Tim Keller, *The Freedom of Self-Forgetfulness*, 10 Publishing, 2017, p. 40)

Matthew and John

The Gospels provide eyewitness testimony of Jesus' life and ministry. Each author includes events and teaching based on his own purpose for writing and his own particular audience. Not surprisingly, each of the four writers gives a detailed account of Jesus' death and resurrection, recognizing that this event is core to the gospel message and Christian faith.

Matthew

Matthew was one of the twelve disciples. He left his work as a tax collector to follow Jesus. His assumption of Jewish customs, extensive quotations from the Old Testament and emphasis on Jesus' descent from King David seems to indicate he wrote his Gospel account primarily for Jewish Christians. His aim was to confirm that Jesus is the Messiah and the fulfilment of Old Testament prophecies.

John

The purpose of John's account was 'that you may believe that Jesus is the Messiah, the Son of God, and that by believing you may have life in his name' (20:31). Chapters 12 – 19 focus exclusively on Jesus' last week – the Last Supper, his final teaching, his prayers for his disciples and all believers, as well as his trial and crucifixion. The key theme of the book is stated in 3:16: 'For God so loved the world that he gave his one and only Son, that whoever believes in him shall not perish but have eternal life.'

Day 5

Read Matthew 27:11–31
Key verses: Matthew 27:27–31

....

Then the governor's soldiers took Jesus into the Praetorium . . . ²⁸They stripped him and put a scarlet robe on him, ²⁹and then twisted together a crown of thorns and set it on his head. They put a staff in his right hand. Then they knelt in front of him and mocked him. 'Hail, king of the Jews!' they said. ³⁰They spat on him, and took the staff and struck him on the head again and again. ³¹After they had mocked him . . . Then they led him away to crucify him.

'Hail, king of the Jews!' the governor's soldiers jeered.

What takes place in verses 27–31 is not standard protocol, but barrack-room humour. The soldiers put a scarlet robe on Jesus, as if he were an emperor or some great leader. They set a crown of thorns on his head, pretending he's a king. Then they put a stick in his hand, pretending it's a sceptre, and kneel in front of him saying, 'Hail, your majesty!' Laughing, they bash the stick against his head again and again.

When they say, 'Hail, King of the Jews!', what they really mean is, 'You're a counterfeit. You're not really the King of the Jews at all!' Pilate makes sure this is the charge written against Jesus because this makes him out to be treasonous against Caesar (verse 37). Their message was: he's a scoundrel and this is what happens to scoundrels. They mean the charge to be deeply ironic. But God knows, Matthew knows and the readers know that Jesus really is the King of the Jews. The soldiers have got it right, and they don't even know it.

The idea of Jesus' kingship has been building from about 1000 BC, when 2 Samuel 7 records the founding of the Davidic dynasty. Over the years there is more revelation about this king. Isaiah 9:6–7 records, 'To us a child is born, to us a son is given . . . he will reign on David's throne.' He is described in spectacular ways: 'Wonderful Counsellor, Mighty God, Everlasting Father, Prince of Peace'.

So there arose a greater and greater expectation of the coming of a messianic figure – an anointed king in David's line who would one day rule. Significantly, the New Testament begins with the origins of Jesus Christ, the son of

Abraham, the son of David. Matthew's Gospel starts with a genealogy, broken up, somewhat artificially, into three series of fourteens, and it is significant that the central fourteen names cover the years of the Old Testament Davidic dynasty. Jesus himself preaches about the 'kingdom of God', and in his parables, like the parable of the sheep and the goats (Matthew 25:31–46), he frequently mentions a king. When you read those narratives carefully, you see that the king cannot be anyone other than Jesus.

A king without soldiers, arms or a geographical domain; headed for death. Jesus is a King with a shatteringly different kingdom: 'The Son of Man did not come to be served, but to serve and to give his life as a ransom for many' (Matthew 20:28). Today Jesus calls his followers to live out the values of his kingdom. One thing this means is that we dare not stand pompously on the authority of our office or focus on ourselves, but rather, passionately seek the good of those in our care.

Day 6

Read Matthew 27:32–44
Key verse: Matthew 27:32

....

As they were going out, they met a man from Cyrene, named Simon, and they forced him to carry the cross.

'We all have our crosses to bear!' we say, referring to an ingrown toenail or an obstreperous mother-in-law. But in the first century, crucifixion was not a joking matter.

Usually the upright of the cross was left in the ground, and the condemned criminal carried the crossbar on his shoulder, out to the place of crucifixion. There you were stripped naked and tied or nailed down to the crossbar. The crossbar was hung up on the upright; your feet were fastened, and thus you were crucified. But Jesus is already so weak, he has been battered so badly he can't even carry the wood on his shoulder, so they have to conscript Simon of Cyrene. It's a picture of his utter weakness, his powerlessness.

The soldiers divide up his clothes and keep watch over him. At an earlier period of the empire they would sometimes just have left people hanging, without guarding them. Once or twice friends had come along and taken the victim down, who would then survive. So now it was imperial policy to leave a quaternion of soldiers (four soldiers) on duty until the crucified person had actually died. Carrying a cross signalled there was no hope at all any more. You were going to die the most excruciating death.

Jesus used this crucifixion image earlier in Matthew's Gospel: 'Whoever wants to be my disciple must deny themselves and take up their cross and follow me. For whoever wants to save their life will lose it, but whoever loses their life for me will find it' (Matthew 16:24–25). For the condemned individual, all that is left is ignominy, pain, shame and death. Jesus says, 'If you want to be my disciple, you have to be similarly crucified every day.'

Of course, for the overwhelming majority of Christians worldwide, Jesus' words have to be taken metaphorically; most of us don't die that way. Jesus speaks so starkly because he understands that what must happen for us to be disciples is, in a sense, equally deeply cutting: we die to ourselves. Jesus himself in the garden cries, 'Not what I will, but what you will!' Genuine disciples of Jesus learn to pray the same thing. We take up our cross. We die willingly, daily, to rise in newness of life, to serve the Lord Christ, who died – literally – on our behalf, emptying himself, burying our guilt so that we might live again.

What are our crosses? They are not simply trials and hardships . . . A cross results from specifically walking in Christ's steps, embracing His life. It comes from bearing disdain because we follow the narrow way of Jesus Christ . . . It comes from living out the business and sexual ethics of Christ in the market place, the community, the family, the world. It comes from standing true in difficult circumstances for the sake of the gospel. Our crosses come from and are proportionate to our dedication to Christ. Difficulties do not indicate cross-bearing, though difficulties for Christ's sake do. Do we have any difficulties because we are closely following Christ?

(Kent Hughes, *Luke*, Crossway Books, 2015, p. 349)

Day 7

Read Matthew 27:32–44
Key verses: Matthew 27:39–40

....

Those who passed by hurled insults at him, shaking their heads ⁴⁰and saying, 'You who are going to destroy the temple and build it in three days, save yourself! Come down from the cross, if you are the Son of God!'

Did Jesus actually say that he would destroy the temple?

It was a dangerous charge, because destroying a temple, even just desecrating one, was a capital offence in the Roman Empire. There were so many religions in the empire that this was one of the ways that the Romans imposed peace. False witnesses reported that Jesus had said this (Matthew 26:61), but the charges didn't stick. In the end, as far as the Roman courts were concerned, the charge was that in claiming to be a king, he was a threat to Caesar.

So, what *had* Jesus said? This is one instance where you get a fuller picture if you read the Gospels together. At the beginning of his ministry John records Jesus as saying, 'Destroy this temple, and I will raise it again in three days' (John 2:19). Neither his opponents nor his disciples understood what he meant. Perhaps their confusion was understandable. Temple-building was a slow process. In Jerusalem you weren't allowed to use a hammer and chisel anywhere within hearing of the temple, which meant that everything had to be cut, measured and brought in without hydraulics – and then put in place. Construction took a long time.

But after Jesus had died and risen again, the disciples remembered his words and believed the Scriptures (John 2:22). They understood he was talking about his own body. The temple was the place where human beings were reconciled to God by the sacrifices that God himself had ordained, such as the sacrifice of Passover, the morning and evening sacrifice, the sacrifice of the Day of Atonement. Jesus now becomes the temple because he becomes the great meeting-place between a holy God and sinful people.

The people think they're being ironic, 'Oh, you're the great temple destroyer and temple builder!' By which they mean, of course, exactly the opposite. 'You are going to destroy the temple and build it in three days? Look at you! You can't do anything!' Their mockery is thick. But there's a deeper irony because God knows, Matthew knows and the reader knows that it's by staying on the cross that Jesus builds the new temple by which sinners like you and me are reconciled to God. The one who is powerless is in fact powerful, and he becomes the great temple that brings sinners and God together precisely by emptying himself and becoming a wretch on a cross.

Christ was all anguish that I may be joy,
cast off that I might be brought in,
trodden down as an enemy
that I might be welcomed as a friend,
surrendered to hell's worst
that I might attain heaven's best,
stripped that I might be clothed,
wounded that I might be healed,
athirst that I might drink,
tormented that I might be comforted,
made a shame that I might inherit glory,
entered darkness that I might have eternal light.
(ed. Arthur Bennett, *Valley of Vision*, Banner of Truth Trust, 2016, p. 76)

Day 8

Read Matthew 27:32–44
Key verses: Matthew 27:41–42

• •

In the same way the chief priests, the teachers of the law and the elders mocked him. [42] *'He saved others,' they said, 'but he can't save himself! He's the king of Israel! Let him come down now from the cross, and we will believe in him.'*

What does the verb 'to save' mean?

If you're a sports fan, it's what you're supposed to do to stop the ball dribbling into the net in a World Cup game. If you're a computer geek, it's what you had better do unless you want to lose an awful lot of data. But what does 'to save' mean in the New Testament? In Matthew 1:21 Joseph is told, 'You are to give him the name Jesus, because he will *save* his people from their sins.'

This announcement provides a grid for how we are supposed to read Matthew's Gospel. So when Jesus teaches in the Sermon on the Mount, he is presenting what the consummated kingdom will be like when he has saved his people from their sins. There will actually be perfection: 'Be perfect as your heavenly Father is perfect.' In chapter 10 when Jesus sends out his disciples, and in chapter 28 when he issues the Great Commission, we learn how Jesus will save his people from their sins through the proclamation of the gospel. This message 'Jesus saves' is in every chapter of the Gospel and ties the entire book together.

Of course, when the chief priests jeered, 'He saved others, but he can't save himself!' they meant to be ironic. 'He can't be much of a saviour to be hanging on the cross, damned by God and human beings both!' But God knows, Matthew knows and the reader knows that there's a deeper irony. It is precisely by not saving himself that he saves others.

If he had stepped down from the cross, the chief priests would have had to backtrack. In one sense, they would have believed. But they wouldn't have been believing in the Son of God who offers his life as a sacrifice, because he wouldn't be offering his life as a sacrifice. It is precisely by staying there that he saves others. When the mockers say, 'He saved others, but he cannot save himself,' they think the 'cannot' is bound up with the nails. But Jesus has already declared in the previous hours: 'Do you think I cannot call on . . . twelve legions of angels?' (Matthew 26:53). A few rusty nails aren't going to mean all that much to twelve legions of angels. No, the 'cannot' is not physical, it's moral.

Jesus is constrained not by might, nails or loss of blood. He is constrained by his passionate commitment to do his Father's will. In that sense, he cannot save himself, and that is how he saves others.

> Heavenly Father, thank you that the Lord Jesus stayed on the cross to save me; not held there by nails but his obedience to you. He suffered the soldiers' beatings, endured the religious leaders' mockery, wore the crown of thorns, and let sinful men crucify him because of his passionate commitment to his Father's will and his enduring love for us – 'Hallelujah, what a Saviour!' (Philip P. Bliss, 1875)

Day 9

Read Matthew 27:38–54
Key verse: Matthew 27:46

....

About three in the afternoon Jesus cried out in a loud voice, 'Eli, Eli, lema sabachthani?' (which means 'My God, my God, why have you forsaken me?').

'He trusts in God. Let God rescue him now,' the religious leaders jeer (verse 43). Full of irony, what they really mean is, 'He can't really trust in God. If he did, God wouldn't have let him go to the cross!' Jesus' anguished cry, 'My God, my God, why have you forsaken me?' almost seems to justify their charges.

But the opposite is true. Jesus is quoting a psalm of David. Throughout Psalm 22 David simultaneously cries to God in the most abject despair, while demonstrating his trust in God. It's not that the despair means that David is not trusting in God. It's precisely in his despair that he trusts God all the more! Jesus understands the meaning of the text, and as David's royal heir, he now uses the same words. He is the Davidic King who is trusting in his heavenly Father as he cries out in a despair even greater than David's.

While he cries out, the heavens become dark, a way of symbolizing that the wrath of God is upon Christ as he goes to the cross. We remember Matthew's words laced throughout his Gospel that have anticipated this event. He speaks of Jesus as the One who will take away our sins, and who came not to be served but to serve and to give his life as a ransom for many (Matthew 1:21; 20:28). Just a few hours earlier on the night that he was betrayed, Jesus himself says that his blood 'is the blood of the new covenant, which is shed for many for the remission of sins' (Matthew 26:28, NKJV).

Jesus knew what he was doing when he went to the cross. He wasn't taken by surprise. But in the bleakness of the hour, as all our sin is upon him, and he feels utterly abandoned and alone, the person of the Godhead who bears our guilt cries out in the most amazingly bleak despair – while simultaneously trusting in God. God knows, Matthew knows and the readers know that it was that trust in God that prompted Jesus to say in the garden, 'Not my will, but yours be done.' Jesus' trust in God took him to this very place.

Jesus cried, 'My God, my God, why have you forsaken me?' so that for all eternity, you wouldn't have to. As the poet Elizabeth Barrett Browning wrote so eloquently,

> Yea, once, Immanuel's orphaned cry his universe
> > hath shaken –
> It went single, echoless, 'My God, I am forsaken!'
> It went up from the Holy lips
> Amid His lost creation,
> That of the lost no son should use
> Those words of desolation.
> (Elizabeth Barrett Browning, 'Cowper's Grave', in *The Complete Poetical Works of Elizabeth Barrett Browning*, BiblioBazaar, 2009, p. 59)

Today, know that in your deepest moments of despair, ill health and grief, God will never forsake you. You can trust him in the darkness, you can cling to him in obedience, because just as at Calvary, he is working his purpose out and he is in control.

Day 10

Read John 19:17–27
Key verses: John 19:17–18

....

Carrying his own cross, he went out to the place of the Skull (which in Aramaic is called Golgotha). [18]*There they crucified him, and with him two others – one on each side and Jesus in the middle.*

Imagine the scene:

Jesus carries his own cross, almost certainly only the cross-piece. Normally the upright was already in place in cities within the empire; crucifixions were depressingly commonplace. He staggers along the road, with help from Simon of Cyrene (Mark 15:21). No doubt overwhelmed with loss of blood from his scourging and beating, he collapses beneath the load.

They come to a small hill called Golgotha. There the soldiers crucify him, which means they would have laid Jesus on that cross-piece, driven a nail through each wrist, right through the central nerve as it runs down the arm. The pain would be unspeakable. Then, with some pulley arrangement, they would attach the cross-piece to the upright, fix it in place, and then the two feet, one on top of the other, would be nailed to the wood.

Hanging there in that position meant the chest cavity was hugely constricted, and so to open it to get breath, you had to pull and push, and the pain would sear through the body. A gasp of breath and then you sink down again, and then another and another. This strange and terrible dance of death went on until the victim, unable any longer to make the effort to breathe, would be mercifully delivered by asphyxiation. People hung on crosses some-times for days. The Roman writer Cicero described it as 'a most cruel and disgusting punishment' (Michael Licona, *The Resurrection of Jesus: A New Historiographical Approach*, IVP, 2010, p. 304).

The Gospel writers do not dwell unduly on the physical agony of the crucifixion, and neither should we. How-ever, it is worth pausing to reflect on the extent of Christ's suffering and what he endured to save us. Because Christ suffered, we can be sure he understands our suffering and stands with us in it.

In the real world of pain, how could one worship a God who was immune to it? I have entered many Buddhist temples in different Asian countries and stood respectfully before the statue of the Buddha, his legs crossed, arms folded, eyes closed, the ghost of a smile playing round his mouth, a remote look on his face, detached from the agonies of the world. But each time after a while I have had to turn away. And in imagination I have turned instead to that lonely, twisted, tortured figure on the cross, nails through hands and feet, back lacerated, limbs wrenched, brow bleeding from thorn-pricks, mouth dry and intolerably thirsty, plunged in Godforsaken darkness. That is the God for me! He laid aside his immunity to pain. He entered our world of flesh and blood, tears and death. He suffered for us. Our sufferings become more manageable in the light of his. There is still a question mark against human suffering, but over it we boldly stamp another mark, the cross that symbolizes divine suffering.

(John Stott, *The Cross of Christ*, IVP, 1986, p. 387)

Day 11

Read John 19:17–27
Key verses: John 19:19–22

· ·

Pilate had a notice prepared and fastened to the cross. It read: JESUS OF NAZARETH, THE KING OF THE JEWS. [20] Many of the Jews read this sign, for the place where Jesus was crucified was near the city, and the sign was written in Aramaic, Latin and Greek. [21] The chief priests of the Jews protested to Pilate, 'Do not write, "The King of the Jews", but that this man claimed to be king of the Jews.'

[22] Pilate answered, 'What I have written, I have written.'

At that moment Jesus looked like a strange king.

Writhing in the darkness – because darkness had fallen upon the whole land – terrible minute upon terrible minute, hour after hour. He was the antithesis of dominion in every sense. But, despite appearances, Jesus is the greatest King. Pilate's sign, 'Here is the King', was written in three languages. Unintentionally appropriate, because Jesus claims the world!

The sign was written in Greek, the language historically associated with the realm of culture. The church at times has turned a jaundiced eye upon all things artistic and creative, but Christ claims the world of culture no less than any other. Human creativity surely is a gift from him who made all things, and these gifts, brought to his feet, can be made a vehicle of praise to him.

'Here is the King' was written in Latin, the language of government, law and institutions. Too often the church has been unwilling to get involved in the messy, sometimes evil world of business, politics and power, but Christ claims this world as his own too. He is able, through lives surrendered to his lordship, to bring the salt and light of his kingdom to the arenas of public life.

The final inscription was written in Aramaic, and Christ claims the world of religion, which that language represents, as his own. He alone is the way to God; he calls us to acknowledge him, and in his name to call the lost millions who follow the empty gods of other religions, to bow before this King, exalted on a cross. Jesus himself promised, 'And I, when I am lifted up from the earth, will draw all people to myself' (John 12:32).

One of the great limitations that have beset human saviours, who over the centuries have dreamed dreams and flung their empires around the world, is that too often they lose sight of the individual. Our little personal universe of hope, pain, struggle and achievement is irrelevant to the great plan. The individual becomes expendable. Not to this King. Jesus rules in all the world, and yet he also comes to us in our personal world; our King is the King of the world.

Jesus was never more kingly than when he was dying to save us. One day his kingship over every sphere of life will be recognized – everyone will bow before him and confess he is Lord (Philippians 2:10–11). Until then we worship him and submit to his rule, praying that others would acknowledge his kingship willingly, while there is still time.

Day 12

Read John 19:17–27
Key verses: John 19:23–27

....

When the soldiers crucified Jesus, they took his clothes, dividing them into four shares, one for each of them, with the undergarment remaining. This garment was seamless, woven in one piece from top to bottom.

24'Let's not tear it,' they said to one another. 'Let's decide by lot who will get it.'

This happened that the scripture might be fulfilled that said,

*'They divided my clothes among them
and cast lots for my garment.'*

So this is what the soldiers did.

25Near the cross of Jesus stood his mother, his mother's sister, Mary the wife of Clopas, and Mary Magdalene. 26When Jesus saw his mother there, and the disciple whom he loved standing nearby, he said to her, 'Woman, here is your son,' [27] *and to the disciple, 'Here is your mother.' From that time on, this disciple took her into his home.*

If this was a scene from a film, the spotlight would be intently focused on Jesus. However, around the cross, some others played minor roles, which John captured in intricate detail. He presents us with four cameos which add to our understanding of what went on that first Good Friday.

Cameo one. Other criminals on each side, Jesus in the middle (verse 18). It is appropriate that, to the very last, Jesus is among sinners.

Cameo two. The Jewish high priests urged Pilate, the Roman governor, to change the sign he had prepared and fastened to the cross: 'Jesus of Nazareth, the King of the Jews' (verse 21). But Pilate would not be pushed any more. (To learn about Pilate's role in Jesus' crucifixion, read John 18:28 – 19:16.) He would not change the truth into a lie.

Cameo three. The soldiers distributed Jesus' belt, sandals, head turban and outer garment among themselves. But his undergarment was rather special; it was seamless, woven in one piece from top to bottom, and so they gambled for it. Psalm 22, written a thousand years before, is fulfilled astonishingly to the very letter: 'They divided my clothes among them and cast lots for my garment.' Such fulfilment of Scripture is an indication of God's presence and sovereignty, even in the midst of all this darkness.

Cameo four. We see the women who cared for Jesus standing near the cross. 'A sword will pierce your soul,' the old man Simeon had said to Mary when she and Joseph took Jesus to the temple for the first time (Luke 2:35). Now that sword was turning. What pain for Mary, for any mother, to be there, and yet, where else would she be? She's there for him. And, in his last moments of life, Jesus ministers to his mother in infinite love, commissioning John to look after her: 'Here is your son; here is your mother.'

If you had been at Calvary that first Good Friday, how would you have responded? What part do you think you would have played? I hope I would have been like that other soldier in Mark 15:39: 'When the centurion, who stood there in front of Jesus, saw how he died, he said, "Surely this man was the Son of God!"'

Day 13

Read John 19:28–37
Key verses: John 19:28–30

....

Later, knowing that everything had now been finished, and so that Scripture would be fulfilled, Jesus said, 'I am thirsty.' [29]A jar of wine vinegar was there, so they soaked a sponge in it, put the sponge on a stalk of the hyssop plant, and lifted it to Jesus' lips. [30]When he had received the drink, Jesus said, 'It is finished.' With that, he bowed his head and gave up his spirit.

What does Jesus mean when he cries out, 'It is finished'?

- *His obedience to his Father's will is finished.* Jesus said, 'My food . . . is to do the will of him who sent me and to finish his work' (John 4:34).

- *His defeat of his Father's enemy is finished.* Jesus triumphed over Satan once and for all. 'Having disarmed the powers and authorities, he made a public spectacle of them, triumphing over them by the cross' (Colossians 2:15).

- *The revealing of his Father's heart is finished.* There is no God behind the back of Jesus, but Jesus reveals all that God is to us. Jesus had said, 'Anyone who has seen me has seen the Father' (John 14:9). He prayed to his Father, 'I have revealed you to those whom you gave me out of the world' (John 17:6). At the cross we see the climax of that revelation. We see how holy God is because he cannot overlook, forget or ignore sin. We also see God's infinite and everlasting love thundering from Calvary across the generations. Look at the cross and tell yourself: this is not just what God thought about me two thousand years ago, but this is exactly what God thinks and feels about me now.

- *The redeeming of the Father's world is finished.* Jesus died in Jerusalem at Passover, a feast commemorating that moment in Egypt when for the liberation of the Israelites a spotless lamb was slain. Now all these centuries later the perfect Lamb of God is slain on the cross and his blood is shed so that we might be free. It is appropriate that this scene ends with Jesus taking a drink and then saying, 'It is finished.' In his death he is taking another cup from the hand of his Father, a cup of wrath and judgement (Isaiah 51:17). He drinks that cup until not a drop is left, and then cries out, 'It is finished.' On the cross Jesus' finished work achieved salvation, full and free, for all his people for ever more.

The Lord Jesus could die on the cross a thousand times, yet no salvation would be accomplished until God in heaven was satisfied . . . If the work of Christ is to be finished, it is essential that it be finished in the estimation of God.

'Is it truly finished?' the Father might be pictured asking himself. 'Did he do all that I sent him to do? Was he perfect in his character and life . . . and – above all – did he really save the sinners I sent him to save?' And on the third day the Father raised him from the dead, so that we might know the estimate he placed on his Son. (Alec Motyer, *Lord is King: Keswick 1979*, STL, 1979, pp. 131–132)

Day 14

Read John 19:28–37
Key verses: John 19:33–37

••

But when they came to Jesus and found that he was already dead, they did not break his legs. ³⁴Instead, one of the soldiers pierced Jesus' side with a spear, bringing a sudden flow of blood and water. ³⁵The man who saw it has given testimony, and his testimony is true. He knows that he tells the truth, and he testifies so that you also may believe. ³⁶These things happened so that the scripture would be fulfilled: 'Not one of his bones will be broken,' ³⁷and, as another scripture says, 'They will look on the one they have pierced.'

Could Jesus simply have been unconscious on the cross?

Many Muslims and others still believe the 'swoon theory', that Jesus did not die on the cross – he simply fainted, or swooned, and was presumed dead. But this is absolute nonsense.

Let's look at the facts.

The Jews were anxious to clear the crosses for Passover, so the soldiers were given permission to break the legs of the crucified. When individuals could no longer push up on the cross and breathe, they expired quickly. By the time the soldiers came to Jesus, they realized he was already dead. To make absolutely sure, they pierced him with a spear. The Roman soldiers knew a dead body when they saw one. That same spear had probably been thrust through dozens before Jesus. Besides which, how could Jesus, having barely escaped death, a few days later have filled the disciples with a radiant conviction that he'd not only come back, but he'd conquered death (see John 20 – 21)? It's impossible. Jesus was dead.

The blood pours from Jesus' side. But there's something else – water. Because Jesus probably died of cardiac arrest, as the final act of taking the world's sin upon him, there is a gathering of fluid around the lungs, and so water flows out. John sees it and knows it is water, the great symbol of the Spirit, the water of life. Jesus talked to Nicodemus about it. He talked to the woman of Samaria about it. He spoke of the Spirit they would receive and, wonderfully, even as Jesus dies, the Spirit is stirring.

These marvellous prophecies from Zechariah 12:10, Psalm 34:20 and Exodus 12, given five hundred, a thousand and thirteen hundred years earlier, are fulfilled to the letter. God is in control; the Spirit is moving.

Jesus truly died, and evil appeared to have triumphed. But, in reality, God's sovereignty was undiminished, and his Spirit was at work. The cross testifies to the unshakeable truth that God is not only in control of dire circumstances, but can use them to further his eternal purposes. Praise God that in our darkest times, in our deepest suffering, he is in control and at work.

> The sovereignty of God is the one impregnable rock to which the suffering human heart must cling. The circumstances surrounding our lives are no accident; they may be the work of evil, but that evil is held firmly within the mighty hand of our sovereign God . . . All evil is subject to Him, and evil cannot touch His children unless He permits it.
>
> (Margaret Clarkson, *Grace Grows Best in Winter*, Eerdmans, 1984, pp. 40–41)

Romans and 1 Corinthians

The apostle Paul was a prolific letter writer. He wrote to churches and individuals on a variety of issues. His letters to the Romans and the Corinthians are significant, not least because they teach us what Jesus' death on the cross means for our salvation and the difference it is to make to our daily lives.

Romans

Paul had always longed to visit Rome. Probably during his third missionary journey, on the way back to Jerusalem with the collection he'd received for the poverty-stricken believers there, Paul wrote to the church in Rome anticipating his visit. To this mixed congregation of Jews and Gentiles he presented God's plan of salvation, rooted in Jesus' death on the cross.

1 Corinthians

1 Corinthians is a response to a letter the church sent Paul (7:1) and a visit he had from concerned members of the congregation (1:11). As such, he sought to address a

number of issues facing the church: challenges to his apostolic authority, division and rivalry among believers, immorality seeping in from the surrounding culture, false teaching about the resurrection, and abuse of communion. Paul wanted believers to understand that the gospel is not just for salvation, but for life – it must have an impact on our character and our conduct.

Day 15

Read Romans 8:28–39
Key verse: Romans 8:30

....

And those he predestined, he also called; those he called, he also justified; those he justified, he also glorified.

Imagine a wedding.

The man says 'I do' and the woman says 'I do', and then the minister pronounces them 'husband and wife'. It's an objective declaration. It is this kind of objective declaration that Paul is talking about when he says in verse 30 that we are 'justified'. As Jesus bore our sins on the cross, God looked at his death and said, 'There is a legal payment for sin, and I am satisfied.' When you believed in Jesus, God saw a legal transaction take place: all Christ's righteousness was credited to you. This doesn't mean that when you put your faith in Jesus, you are perfect in character. It means that you are suddenly perfect in status. Like a marriage, it is a declaration, not a transformation.

The technical term for attributing righteousness is 'impute'. The Bible says that if I have called on the Lord, put my faith in him, God has credited to me, imputed to me, not only forgiveness, but righteousness.

So, being justified means:

- *You can be sure of your salvation*. Your salvation is not dependent on how you feel or perform. God's declaration is based on the death of Jesus.

- *You can be sure you are accepted by God*. Acceptance in society is based on how you look and succeed. The hunger to be accepted is never satisfied because you can never sustain the position of beauty and success – it is a momentary thing. In contrast, God's acceptance of the believer is fixed, secure, profound and for ever.

- *You can be sure of the final verdict*. Christianity is very simple. You say 'no' to Christ, and one day he will say 'no' to you. You say 'yes' to Christ, and one day he will say 'yes' to you. It is not pride to say, 'I am going to heaven'; it is pride to doubt God's verdict on your life when Christ has died and God has spoken.

- *You can be sure God is for you*. Isaiah 30:18 says, 'Yet the LORD longs to be gracious to you; therefore he will rise up to show you compassion. For the LORD is a God of justice. Blessed are all who wait for him!' Suffering does not have an attack built into it. God may use suffering to shape and transform, but it is wielded by God who works for your good and loves you through to the end.

If you are dealing with doubts and difficulties, remind yourself of the truth of the gospel. Meditate on the certainties of what God's declaration of being 'justified' means for your life. Cling to the truth that your salvation is sure, you are accepted by God, the final verdict is not in doubt, and God is for you.

Day 16

Read 1 Corinthians 1:17 – 2:5
Key verses: 1 Corinthians 1:17–18

....

For Christ did not send me to baptise, but to preach the gospel – not with wisdom and eloquence, lest the cross of Christ be emptied of its power. [18]*For the message of the cross is foolishness to those who are perishing, but to us who are being saved it is the power of God.*

How can we get right with God?

Other religions say, 'Here is what you must *do*. Go to the temple, church or mosque. Perform religious duties. Give money away. Be nice to those who are in trouble.' But the Christian message says, 'No. You will never be able to *do* enough.' There's a massive barrier of sin that cuts off sinful people from the holy God. We will never be able to *do* enough to get over that barrier. Yet wonderfully, uniquely, it has all been done for us. Christ himself, through his death on the cross, has blazed a trail through that great barrier of sin, and he's taken upon himself all the things that we've done wrong, as well as the judgement of his Father, so that we might be forgiven.

This message of the cross is rejected by most. In terms of human wisdom, it is foolishness (1:18). But the weakness of the message of the cross has divine mighty power (verse 17). One day we will look around God's throne and see millions from every tribe, race and nation, there because of the message of the cross. In the meantime, how are we going to reach our friends, neighbours and those around the world with the good news of Christ? Are we going to rely on church planting, new buildings, seeker courses or brilliant speakers? Those things might help, but they're just a means to the end. We need to rely on the message of the cross. That is, the power of God.

Of course, this is not the message people are asking for. Just as the Jews demand miraculous signs (verse 22), there are still those who say, 'Go on, prove God. Unless you prove him to me, I won't believe in him.' The Greeks looked for wisdom, and there are millions today who say, 'Just impress me with something that makes sense and fits with the mindset of the world.' It is tempting to present a message that is soft on sin, judgement and the uniqueness of Christ, but strong on affirmation: 'You're wonderful; God loves you just as you are!' That message might be popular, but it's not powerful. Loads of people might come and hear it, but it saves none. We need to follow the example of the apostle Paul: 'We preach Christ crucified: a stumbling block to Jews and foolishness to Gentiles, but to those whom God has called, both Jews and Greeks, Christ the power of God and the wisdom of God' (verses 23–24).

Could it be that our evangelism is powerless because we have compromised the message? Pray for gospel conversations that you will have this week with family and friends, at church on Sunday, in the gym or at the school gate. Ask God to be at work as, in his strength, you present the message of 'Christ crucified'.

Day 17

Read 1 Corinthians 1:17 – 2:5

Key verses: 1 Corinthians 2:2–5

....

For I resolved to know nothing while I was with you except Jesus Christ and him crucified. ³I came to you in weakness with great fear and trembling. ⁴My message and my preaching were not with wise and persuasive words, but with a demonstration of the Spirit's power, ⁵so that your faith might not rest on human wisdom, but on God's power.

'All God's giants have been weak people' (Vaughan Roberts, *True Spirituality*, IVP, 2011).

Those were the words of Hudson Taylor, the great nineteenth-century missionary to China. And he was right. Paul explains in 1 Corinthians 1:27, 'God chose the foolish things of the world to shame the wise; God chose the weak things of the world to shame the strong.' Choosing weak people is God's deliberate strategy. Why? 'So that no one may boast before him' (verse 29). It's quite clear that the power of God, bringing people to conversion, has worked through weak people. No one will exalt those weak people and say, 'Aren't you marvellous!' But they will glory in God, so that no one may boast before him.

When Paul first visited Corinth, he knew that he'd be much more acceptable if he gave them what they wanted: human wisdom. But quite deliberately, having thought it through, he resisted that temptation: 'When I came to you, I did not come with elegance or [superior] wisdom as I proclaimed to you the testimony about God. For I resolved to know nothing while I was with you except Jesus Christ and him crucified' (2:1–2). Paul was fearful speaking to the Corinthians because he knew that the world mocks and hates the message of the cross (verse 3). And yet a church was founded there by a weak man proclaiming a weak message in the power of the Spirit of God.

The devil tells us that if we want to see people becoming Christians, we need to pay attention to human personalities, techniques and oratory. His message is seductive: 'You want to reach the world, don't you? You want to see people saved! They're really not going to listen to you.' Paul's testimony is that God's power is seen in our weakness. Spiritual power is unleashed when weak men and women speak out the message of Christ and his cross.

If we are not fit to hold such a glorious treasure as the gospel, then why in the world would God entrust it to us?! 'To show that the surpassing power belongs to God and not to us.' We are unfit, breakable, disposable vessels, and God has decided to use our weakness to display his power and love. A jar of clay may be cracked in a few places, making it unusable in the world's eyes, but God sees these deficiencies as a means to pour out and reveal more of himself.

The pastor and author Mark Dever hits the nail on the head when he says,

When we rely on God, and God shows himself to be faithful, he gets the glory. This is what he has always intended. He does not intend us to be strong, self-reliant and without need of turning to him . . . He intends for us to be weak and oppressed, and then to turn and rely on him, because then he can provide what we need and thereby be glorified.

(Mark Dever, *The Message of the New Testament*, p. 203; quoted in Kirsten Wetherell and Sarah Walton, *Hope When it Hurts*, The Good Book Company, 2017, pp. 26–27)

Philippians, Colossians and Titus

Philippians

Paul is writing to the church in the Roman colony of Philippi to thank them for their financial gift and update them on his work. He writes about a wide range of issues relating to Christian living. He exhorts them to 'rejoice in the Lord' (4:4), grow in love, and stand firm in the face of persecution. Chapter 2:6–11, perhaps an early Christian song, describes Jesus' humility going to the cross and his subsequent exaltation by his Father. Paul is not just providing theological information, but urging believers to share Christ's mindset and strive for unity in the church.

Colossians

The church at Colossae was founded when Epaphras, a convert of Paul's from Ephesus, took the gospel back to his home town (1:7–8). Heresy had invaded this young church and Paul wrote from his prison cell in Rome, or perhaps Ephesus, to help these new believers hold fast to the truth of the gospel. His letter emphasizes the complete adequacy of Christ, who is the image of God, the head of the church, the first to be resurrected from the dead, and the Reconciler of all things. He reminds the Colossians what they once were, and the difference Jesus' death has made for their present and future.

Titus

After Paul's release from his first imprisonment in Rome, he and Titus briefly visited Crete. Paul asked Titus to stay on the island to establish the church and appoint elders (1:5). It was not easy to be a Christian on Crete, as the island was rife with immorality, gluttony and laziness (1:12). Paul is keen to remind these new converts that accepting the grace of the gospel results in a change of lifestyle. In a depraved society, believers are to be recognized by their holy living. Titus is to teach the people to know and do 'what is good' (1:8, 16; 2:3, 7, 14; 3:1, 8, 14).

Day 18

Read Philippians 2:1–18
Key verses: Philippians 2:5–8

....

In your relationships with one another, have the same mindset as Christ Jesus:

> *⁶who, being in very nature God,*
>   *did not consider equality with God something*
>   *to be used to his own advantage;*
> *⁷rather, he made himself nothing*
>   *by taking the very nature of a servant,*
>   *being made in human likeness.*
> *⁸And being found in appearance as a man,*
>   *he humbled himself*
>   *by becoming obedient to death –*
>   *even death on a cross!*

Is disunity and rivalry in a church and grumbling among Christians really that serious? Surely it isn't as serious as doctrinal heresy?

Paul's emphatic answer is: 'Yes, it is!' It is so serious that he urges the believers in Philippi to tackle their infighting and dissent (Philippians 1:15, 17; 2:14; 4:2) by adopting the same 'mindset as Christ'. Jesus plunged downwards from the heights of the Godhead. He was in very nature God, but made himself nothing, humbling himself to become a man, and more than that, to be a suffering servant who died on a cross.

Sharing the mindset of Christ means we too must travel the way of the cross. We don't move on from the message of the cross as soon as we become Christians, but rather, it must shape our lives more and more. That's why Paul retold the gospel to these Philippian believers. He did the same thing when he wrote to Titus to remind the converts in Crete to show humility to all. The believers were behaving as if they were superior to the non-Christians around them. To help them see they were no better than the non-Christians, but were simply forgiven, Paul goes back to the cross to teach them how to live. He explains, 'At one time we too were foolish, disobedient, deceived and enslaved by all kinds of passions and pleasures . . . But when the kindness and love of God our Saviour appeared, he saved us' (Titus 3:3–5). In Titus 3:4–7 Paul reminds them of the gospel and what the cross has achieved.

The apostle Peter also preaches to believers about the cross. In 1 Peter 2:24 he states, '"He himself bore our sins" in his body on the cross, so that we might die to sins and live for righteousness.' Why is Peter reminding Christians that they are saved through the cross of Christ? Because he is struggling with the issue: 'How can I get people who are employed to serve faithfully in the workplace?' Throughout the letters of the New Testament we find issues of Christian conduct resolved by returning to the message of the cross.

Gossip, family feuds, complaints about leaders, rotas, sermons . . . all are accepted, even expected, in our churches. But it shouldn't be this way. Jesus died to reconcile us to God and to each other. The cross makes reconciliation possible, and shows us how it is achieved. As you serve alongside other believers, meet as a home group or talk with a Christian friend over coffee, what does it look like for the cross to shape your interactions and for you to share the mindset of Christ?

Day 19

Read Philippians 2:1–30
Key verse: Philippians 2:12

. . . .

Therefore, my dear friends, as you have always obeyed – not only in my presence, but now much more in my absence – continue to work out your salvation with fear and trembling . . .

What does Paul mean, 'continue to work out your salvation'?

He is not saying you have to save yourself. The cross saves us. But he is saying that we need to work out what it means to adopt a cross-shaped life. In verses 12–30 he gives us three examples of lives shaped by the cross:

* *Himself*. Paul says, 'Even if I am being poured out like a drink offering on the sacrifice and service coming from your faith, I am glad and rejoice with all of you' (verse 17). When the contents of a bottle are poured out, it empties itself and eventually there is nothing left. Paul is pouring out his life in service to God and

others, reminding us of Jesus who 'made himself nothing' (verse 7).

- *Timothy.* Paul remarks, 'I have no one else like him [Timothy], who will show genuine concern for your welfare. For everyone looks out for their own interests, not those of Jesus Christ' (verses 20–21). Timothy was sharing the mindset of Christ as he overlooked his own interests for the sake of others (verses 4–5).

- *Epaphroditus.* Paul urges the Philippians to welcome and honour Epaphroditus because 'he almost died for the work of Christ' (verse 30). He was being shaped by the cross to the extent that he was prepared to risk his life in the service of others. Epaphroditus reminds us of Christ, who humbled himself, going all the way to the cross to give up his life for us.

The apostle does not see the rivalries and dissensions in church life and just cry, 'Work it out!' He portrays the cross of Christ and says, 'This is the way.' He gives us examples of humility, service, suffering and sacrifice, lives shaped by the cross of the Lord Jesus Christ. But more than that, he reminds us that though we stumble and fail, God is at work in us to will and to act according to his good purpose (verse 13). By the power of the Holy Spirit, God will help us make the cross-shaped life more and more of a reality.

Take to heart God's promise that as you live this cross-shaped life, you will shine like a star in the night sky (verses 15–16) – your life authenticating the gospel message to unbelievers; your transformation proving the gospel is true and God is at work.

Use the ACTS acronym to guide your prayers:

- *Adoration*. Worship Christ for his humility, coming to earth to die on a cross for our sake.
- *Confession*. Confess the particular ways you have failed to live a cross-shaped life this week.
- *Thanksgiving*. Thank God for Paul, Timothy, Epaphroditus and the men and women he has put into your life who are godly examples of cross-shaped living.
- *Supplication*. Ask for Holy Spirit power to live the way of the cross in all your dealings today.

Day 20

Read Colossians 1:15–20
Key verses: Colossians 1:19–20

....

For God was pleased to have all his fullness dwell in him, ²⁰and through him to reconcile to himself all things, whether things on earth or things in heaven, by making peace through his blood, shed on the cross.

That God, in Christ, should achieve reconciliation by something he did in his physical body is as revolutionary a concept now as it was in the first century.

What did Jesus do?

He forgave us all our sins, having cancelled the charge of our legal indebtedness, which stood against us and condemned us; he has taken it away, nailing it to the cross. And having disarmed the powers and authorities, he made a public spectacle of them, triumphing over them by the cross.
(Colossians 2:13–15)

Paul talks about the death of Jesus as a victory over the dark powers of this age. What gives these powers and authorities influence over us? It's our guilt and sin that allow the devil to accuse us before God (Revelation 12:10). But the debt we owe God because we have broken his law has been taken by the Lord Jesus and nailed to the cross. Jesus has taken on himself what was against us. He who was without sin was made sin for us (2 Corinthians 5:21). As I see my sin nailed to the cross, I see everything that was written against me nailed to that cross with him, in him, on him. The devil no longer has anything he can say.

Paul can write to the Romans, 'Who will bring any charge against those whom God has chosen? . . . Who condemns? No one. Christ Jesus who died – more than that, who was raised to life – is at the right hand of God and is also interceding for us' (Romans 8:33–34). There is only a victorious Jesus because there is a sin-bearing Jesus. There is only freedom for us from the powers of darkness because Jesus has paid the penalty for our sin, bearing sin in his own body on the tree. By doing that, he's reconciled us to God, by his blood on the cross.

So don't let anyone make you feel guilty: guilt is banished because the Lord Jesus took our place. And don't let anyone disqualify you from Christian service or fellowship with God, because the Lord Jesus Christ guarantees your right standing with God and your firm relationship with him. That's how effective his cross is.

Take a step back, take in the panoramic view. Not only does Jesus' death reconcile you to God, but there is nothing in the universe outside the range of God's reconciling work in Christ, accomplished on the cross (Colossians 1:20). You and I are reconciled to God, but so is the whole of the cosmos. Christ, the fullness of God, who was there in the beginning, who created and sustains all things, will through his death on the cross usher in the new creation. Praise God today for the power of the cross and the glorious message of the gospel.

Day 21

Read Colossians 1:15–23
Key verses: Colossians 1:21–22

• •

Once you were alienated from God and were enemies in your minds because of your evil behaviour. 22But now he has reconciled you by Christ's physical body through death to present you holy in his sight, without blemish and free from accusation.

Don't you love hearing testimonies or stories of how people came to put their trust in Christ?

In these verses Paul is giving the Colossians' testimony for them. He describes what they were like before they came to Christ (verse 21). 'Alienated from God' means separated and distanced from him. 'Enemies in your minds' is having a mindset of hostility to God. 'Evil behaviour' indicates living lives which were rebellious to him. Paul's strong language makes us wonder if there was something particularly bad about these Colossians. But there's no evidence in the letter that the Colossians were worse than anybody else. These are just the terms the apostle Paul uses to speak about people before they come to faith: 'All of us also lived among them at one time, gratifying the cravings of our flesh and following its desires and thoughts. Like the rest, we were by nature deserving of wrath' (Ephesians 2:3; see also Romans 8:7).

According to the Bible, we don't just need a bit of moral improvement, we have a sinful mindset and are hostile to God, and that's why we desperately need a Saviour. In his autobiography, *Surprised by Joy*, C. S. Lewis described the first time he looked into his own heart:

> For the first time I examined myself with a seriously prac-
> tical purpose. And there I found what appalled me: a
> zoo of lusts, a bedlam of ambitions, a nursery of fears,
> a harem of fondled hatreds. My name was Legion
> (Collins, 2016, p. 263)

Even if we can't think of a time when we weren't a Christian, the Bible says we still have a 'sinful nature' (Romans 7:25). Imagine what we would be like if it weren't for the work of the Spirit of God within us. We'd be alienated from God. That doesn't just mean us keeping God out of the picture, but God, in response to our hostility to him, separating himself from us.

However, Paul says, God has 'reconciled' us (Colossians 1:22). God took the initiative to deal with the consequences of our sin, and turned his face back towards us as Jesus died on the cross and bore the penalty for our sins. Then he sent his Holy Spirit to turn us round so we were in a situation of reconciliation with him. Paul takes us to the cross. He's not talking about a concept; he's talking about a real historical event. Salvation is not us turning over a new leaf. It's Jesus dying, bearing our sins, that we might be forgiven and reconciled to God.

Our reconciliation to God is permanent and eternal. Because Christ accomplished it for us, there is no possibility it can ever be undone. Though we continue, even as believers, to do those things that in themselves deserve God's displeasure, we can never revert to a state of divine alienation. For the sake of Christ, God will always accept us. And even when God deems it necessary to discipline us for persistent disobedience, He always does so out of love to restore us to the way of obedience (see Hebrews 12:4–11).

(Jerry Bridges, *The Gospel for Real Life*, NavPress, 2002, p. 96)

Day 22

Read Colossians 1:15–23
Key verses: Colossians 1:21–22

....

Once you were alienated from God and were enemies in your minds because of your evil behaviour. [22] *But now he has reconciled you by Christ's physical body through death to present you holy in his sight, without blemish and free from accusation.*

Are you reticent about sharing the story of how you came to faith?

Some of us shy away from telling our testimony because it seems too uninteresting or mundane. You may have been saved as a child, and perhaps you don't have a dramatic conversion story. But every Christian's testimony is powerful. We were once alienated from God, but when we put our trust in Christ, our sins were forgiven, fully and freely.

At the cross God 'has reconciled you by Christ's physical body through death to present you *holy in his sight*'. Paul could have finished there, couldn't he? Present you holy in his sight, just as if you'd never sinned – but he goes on: 'without blemish'. The idea is of something completely unstained, no sign of a mark at all. Perfect. Imagine a car when you pick it up from the showroom; there are no scratches on the bodywork at all. Gradually, over the years, the blemishes pile up. In God's sight we are absolutely without blemish *and* free from accusation. There's no possibility that we could be held to account for our sins before the holy God, because he has dealt with them entirely. The devil, who loves to accuse us of our sins, has no ground to stand on because our sins have been wiped away by Christ's sacrifice. All our sin – past, present and future – has been dealt with at Calvary. Every skeleton in the cupboard that you worry about has been forgiven.

In these verses Paul is retelling the Colossians' story. He describes what they were before they came to Christ, and what they are now because of Jesus' work on the cross. These believers have been saved from alienation from God into this marvellous reconciled relationship, from which no one can separate them. In verses 13–14 Paul tells their testimony in another way: 'For he has rescued us from the dominion of darkness and brought us into the kingdom of the Son he loves, in whom we have redemption, the forgiveness of sins.'

Because of what Jesus did on the cross this can be our story too, if we trust in him.

Your testimony may not seem very glamorous or exciting. You may not even remember the exact moment when you trusted in Christ. But don't let that stop you telling other people about what God has done for you. He has brought you from death to life, from alienation to reconciliation, from sinner to saved. Many other religions and life philosophies can change your life for the better, but only the gospel can reconcile you to God and 'present you holy in his sight . . . free from accusation' (verse 22). Don't reduce your testimony to how God has made you more fulfilled and given you a purpose. Put the focus on the Lord Jesus, his cross and the message of the gospel, and your testimony will never seem mundane again.

Day 23

Read Colossians 1:15–23
Key verses: Colossians 1:22–23

....

But now he has reconciled you by Christ's physical body through death to present you holy in his sight, without blemish and free from accusation – ²³*if you continue in your faith, established and firm, and do not move from the hope held out in the gospel. This is the gospel that you heard and that has been proclaimed to every creature under heaven, and of which I, Paul, have become a servant.*

Do you realize just how good the good news is?

The Colossians were being bombarded by some unhelpful teaching, so Paul wrote to urge them not to move, not to be dissuaded, from the gospel (verse 23). We have to read through the letter to try and work out what's going on (2:2, 8), but it seems this teaching can best be summarized under the heading of 'gospel plus' (2:16). These were not woolly liberals, but zealous people saying, 'Yes, what you've heard is all very good, but you need this extra thing in order to lead a godly life.'

Paul responds by saying that, in Christ, you have everything you need. Jesus' absolute sufficiency is the powerful message throughout the letter (see 1:15–18). If I add to the gospel, I'm really taking away from it because I'm saying that who Jesus is, and what he's done, are not sufficient for me to live a godly life.

Of course, there's always room for growth in the Christian life. It is a tremendous battle to grow to be more like Christ, but it's a great mistake to think that we need something more than Christ to be saved or to be sanctified. Christian history is littered with people who have made these kinds of suggestions. Some argue for special religious rituals. Others promote asceticism, or harsh treatment of the body (2:23). Yet others promote a kind of elitism: 'You've got to join *our* church or *our* group. We're the only ones who've really got it.'

It's very damaging when this kind of 'gospel plus' practice goes on in churches, because when we speak to non-Christians about Christ, they automatically think we are wanting to make them religious rather than give them good news. But Paul has much better news: Jesus has done everything necessary to put us right with the Father.

There is no other gospel – Jesus' saving blood is the only place of atonement for our sins, and our only ground for hope before a holy God.

Are you personally persuaded by the absolute sufficiency of Jesus' death on the cross? Get this matter settled in your heart, because it is like a mainspring in a clock – it drives and motivates our Christian gratitude and obedience. It also helps us not to be nibbled away at by the devil. When he reminds us of our sins, we can look to that empty cross and remember the Saviour who has paid the price in full.

> What an unspeakable gift we have been given through the perfect sacrifice of God's own Son, Jesus Christ. Hence, every single Christian should be filled with gratitude. No matter what our age, race, culture, language, social status, or life circumstances, all Christians should be known as characteristically grateful people. We, above all [other] humans, have overwhelming cause to be thankful.
>
> (Mary Mohler, *Growing in Gratitude*, The Good Book Company, 2018, p. 15)

Day 24

Read Titus 2:11–14

Key verses: Titus 2:13–14

....

We wait for the blessed hope – the appearing of the glory of our great God and Saviour, Jesus Christ, [14]who gave himself for us to redeem us from all wickedness and to purify for himself a people that are his very own, eager to do what is good.

Why did Jesus have to die?

Paul says Jesus 'gave himself for us'. In Galatians 2:20 he makes it even more personal: the Lord Jesus 'loved *me* and gave himself for *me*'. Why?

Christ 'gave himself to redeem us'. The word 'redemption' comes from the marketplace, where slaves were purchased for a price. Jesus paid the price for our sins, purchased our salvation, through his death on the cross. This theme runs throughout all Paul's writing. Galatians 1:4 reminds us, 'He gave himself for our sins', as does

Ephesians 5:2: 'He gave himself up for us.' Peter says that we were once enslaved, committed to an empty way of life, and then at just the right moment – as Paul says in Romans 5:6 – God sent Christ to be our Saviour: 'For you know that it was not with perishable things such as silver or gold that you were redeemed from the empty way of life handed down to you from your ancestors, but with the precious blood of Christ' (1 Peter 1:18–19). Jesus' death purchased our redemption. His death was voluntary – he was not coerced by his Father; it was sub-stitutionary – he took my place; and it was propitiatory – it satisfied God's wrath.

From all eternity God planned to purchase your redemp-tion. But we have not been purchased to sit on a shelf and be dusted. We are now 'in Christ', and we are to be pure: 'For the grace of God has appeared that offers salvation to all people. It teaches us to say "No" to ungodliness and worldly passions, and to live self-controlled, upright and godly lives' (Titus 2:11–12). Our redemption is the foundational truth that motivates this practical holiness: 'You are not your own; you were bought at a price. Therefore honour God with your bodies' (1 Corinthians 6:19–20).

Jesus is our kinsman-redeemer with the right to redeem us – made like us in every way, yet without sin (see Hebrews 4:15). He has the resources to redeem us – possessing all authority over nature and nations, disease and demons, sin and Satan, suffering and death. Finally, He has the resolve to redeem us. His resolve drove Him to take responsibility for our sin, enduring the wrath of God that we deserve, so that through faith in Him, we might no longer be outcasts separated from God, but instead we might be called sons and daughters of God. (David Platt, *Counter Culture*, Tyndale House, 2015, p. 104)

Thank God for such a costly redemption, and today respond by living in grateful obedience:

May these words of my mouth and this meditation
    of my heart
  be pleasing in your sight,
  LORD, my Rock and my Redeemer.
(Psalm 19:14)

Day 25

Read Titus 2:11–14

Key verses: Titus 2:13–14

. . . .

We wait for the blessed hope – the appearing of the glory of our great God and Saviour, Jesus Christ, [14]who gave himself for us to redeem us from all wickedness and to purify for himself a people that are his very own, eager to do what is good.

Jesus died to make you his. He didn't just die to 'redeem us *from* all wickedness', he died to 'purify *for* himself a people'.

From eternity God's purpose was to have a people of his own, and repentant sinners are privileged to be part of that people. We only need to listen to Jesus' preaching to learn about God's plan. For example, in John 6, Jesus says, 'All those the Father gives me will come to me, and whoever comes to me I will never drive away . . . And this is the will of him who sent me, that I shall lose none of all those he has given me, but raise them up at the last day'

(John 6:37, 39). Jesus' prayers also reveal God's plan: 'Father, I want those you have given me to be with me where I am, and to see my glory' (John 17:24).

There was no one more surprised at Saul's conversion than Saul of Tarsus himself. But God was not surprised. He said to Ananias: 'This man is my chosen instrument to proclaim my name to the Gentiles and their kings and to the people of Israel' (Acts 9:15). In the same way, you have not been purchased indiscriminately. God's purpose for your life is constrained and kept safe by God's eternal will.

If we are Jesus' 'very own' people, that means we don't belong to anyone else. Our hearts, minds, desires, motives are to be set apart for him, and this has consequences in our work places, homes and schools. Our salvation is meant to make a difference: 'At one time we too were foolish, disobedient, deceived and enslaved by all kinds of passions and pleasures. We lived in malice and envy, being hated and hating one another. But when the kindness and love of God our Saviour appeared, he saved us . . .' (Titus 3:3–4).

The problem is that today the church is at pains to tell the world that we're no different from it. We are like the world in its need, but we're not to be like the world in its sin. The danger is that we become like it in its sin, and so we have nothing to say to its needs.

'They will be my people and I will be their God' is the refrain which began in the Old Testament (see Exodus 6:7; Ezekiel 36:26–28; 37:27; Jeremiah 32:38), and will reach a crescendo in the new heavens and new earth:

> Look! God's dwelling place is now among the people, and he will dwell with them. They will be his people, and God himself will be with them and be their God.
> (Revelation 21:3)

Jesus died to make us his 'very own people', and we are now caught up in God's glorious purpose. As you go about your day, remember – you belong to God. Let that truth sink deep into your heart. Pray also that your church family would grasp this truth, and together you would strive to be people of integrity, authenticity and purity, living unashamedly in obedience to God's Word.

Day 26

Read Titus 2:11–14
Key verses: Titus 2:13–14

....

We wait for the blessed hope – the appearing of the glory of our great God and Saviour, Jesus Christ, [14]who gave himself for us to redeem us from all wickedness and to purify for himself a people that are his very own, eager to do what is good.

Has Jesus' death on the cross so gripped you that you are passionate about living a God-honouring, self-giving life? Has it profoundly shaped your values and priorities?

We have been redeemed to be God's own people and to do 'good'. Doing what is 'good' (verse 14) has been Paul's message throughout this letter. The older women are to 'teach what is good' (2:3). 'Similarly, encourage the young men to be self-controlled. In everything set them an example by doing what is good' (2:6–7). In 3:1 Paul urges these believers to be 'ready to do whatever is good'. In 3:8 he says, 'I want you to stress these things, so that those who have trusted in God may be careful to devote themselves to doing what is good', because that is how these individuals will be distinguished from those who 'claim to know God, but by their actions they deny him. They are detestable, disobedient and unfit for doing anything good' (1:16). What a disaster! To claim to know God and yet to be useless for him.

But Paul's emphasis here is not only on doing good, but on being '*eager* to do what is good'. The word here is translated 'zealous, devoted'. We are to say 'no' to worldly passions, but we're not to be passionless. What a tragedy a passionless church is – insipid and bland – when Jesus said we are to be involved and bold.

Are you useful to God? Do your actions affirm that you know God? Do they point believers and unbelievers to Jesus?

When our efforts go unnoticed or unrewarded, when there is no obvious fruit for our labours, we can easily become disillusioned and weary of doing good. If your zeal is fading, go back to Calvary, spend time at the cross. Jesus' death is the grounds for our devotion; he is our motivation. Serve others, be devoted to them, seek out opportunities, and be willing to sacrifice to bring good to others – but do it all with your eyes firmly fixed on Christ. We do good 'to' others, but we don't ultimately do it 'for' them – it is Christ we are serving. Let's learn to say with Paul, 'We make it our goal to please him' (2 Corinthians 5:9).

Today press on, eager to do good: 'Always give yourselves fully to the work of the Lord, because you know that your labour in the Lord is not in vain' (1 Corinthians 15:58).

Hebrews and 1 John

Hebrews

We don't know who wrote the book of Hebrews, but we do know why it was written. In the face of persecution, some Jewish Christians were drifting away from the gospel. Unbelief had crept in, they were not making spiritual progress and had given up meeting together. Like the previous generation of Israelites in the desert, they were in danger of facing God's judgement. The writer made it clear that returning to the comfortable ways of Judaism was not an option, because Christ's coming had changed the spiritual landscape for ever. Christ was God's full and final revelation; he completes Israel's history, law, ceremonial rituals and priesthood. This book urges believers to persevere in the faith, by pointing them to Christ's absolute supremacy in divine revelation and his absolute sufficiency in Christian experience: 'fix your thoughts . . . [and fix] your eyes on Jesus' (Hebrews 3:1; 12:2).

1 John

In his later years, John, Jesus' beloved disciple, was pastor of the church at Ephesus. It seems that this letter was probably a circular written to the other churches in the province of Asia. John was primarily writing to combat the early signs of Gnosticism. This heresy taught that the spirit was entirely good, and matter, the body, was entirely bad. The teaching had three main consequences – Jesus' humanity was denied; salvation was believed to be an escape from the body and the acquisition of special knowledge rather than having faith in Christ; and lack of morality was rife because it didn't matter what you did with your body. John wrote as an eyewitness to testify to the incarnation of Christ, and to assure the believers of their salvation. He wanted the Christians to know that they could base their whole lives on the truths of the gospel, and that this was the source of true joy (1:4).

Day 27

Read Hebrews 10:8–18
Key verses: Hebrews 10:8–10

....

First he said, 'Sacrifices and offerings, burnt offerings and sin offerings you did not desire, nor were you pleased with them' – though they were offered in accordance with the law. ⁹Then he said, 'Here I am, I have come to do your will.' He sets aside the first to establish the second. ¹⁰And by that will, we have been made holy through the sacrifice of the body of Jesus Christ once for all.

We realize that Jesus could have died a thousand times and promised a thousand pardons and still not accomplished our salvation. Because, if God's wrath was not satisfied, then Jesus' death on the cross was pointless.

But the writer to the Hebrews assures us that Calvary does indeed satisfy God because it was his idea. Verse 10 explains that the salvation of sinners arises out of the will of God. In his first sermon Peter says that the crucifixion took place by God's 'deliberate plan and foreknowledge' (Acts 2:23). Wicked men crucified Jesus, and nothing will ever absolve them of the responsibility of doing that, but Jesus went to the cross because of the deliberate plan and foreknowledge of God. Our salvation is rooted in his will. As Isaiah prophesied, on the cross the sins of the world – past, present and future – are gathered up by the Father and laid upon his Son: 'The LORD has laid on him the iniquity of us all' (Isaiah 53:6; see Day 1).

We also know that Jesus' death satisfies God because of the welcome he gave to Jesus. Would God have welcomed Jesus to sit at his right hand, that place of exaltation (verse 12), if he had failed to accomplish his Father's purpose? The Holy Spirit also testifies that God is satisfied (verse 15). No member of the Trinity can keep silent on this theme! The substance of God's testimony is: 'Their sins and lawless acts I will remember no more' (verse 17).

Yes, God's wrath is wholly satisfied. And to demonstrate this, on Good Friday he tore apart the veil of the temple (Matthew 27:51). The separation between God and man was now over, and God was inviting sinners into his presence through the precious blood shed on Calvary. Today we can come boldly into God's presence in the full assurance of faith, because of the Christ of Calvary.

Heavenly Father, thank you that today I can come into your presence because my sin has been paid for and your wrath has been satisfied. Lord Jesus, thank you for obeying your Father's will, dying in my place, taking the punishment I deserved. May I be forever grateful for this amazing 'grace in which we now stand' (Romans 5:1–2).

In his death on the cross, Christ becomes the place of refuge, the place in the world where the full wrath of God has already been spent. Therefore, to stand in Christ is to stand in a place where the wrath of God will never be felt, because it has already been there.

(Rory Shiner, *One Forever*, Matthias Media, 2013)

Day 28

Read Hebrews 10:11–18
Key verses: Hebrews 10:11–12

. . . .

Day after day every priest stands and performs his religious duties; again and again he offers the same sacrifices, which can never take away sins. ¹²*But when this priest had offered for all time one sacrifice for sins, he sat down at the right hand of God.*

'I haven't sat down all day!'

When we hear someone say this, we get the message that they have been busy. Sometimes you can be busy while sitting down, but generally speaking, if you're standing, you're busy, and sitting down is a signal that you have finished for the day. The writer to the Hebrews depicts the Lord Jesus as sitting down for that very reason – he has finished his work.

He will never again stretch out his hands to be nailed to a cross. He doesn't need to make another sacrifice because this one was effective for sins – *plural* – the sum total of the sins of all the sinners whom he came to save. The Bible gives three categories of sin: outward acts of wrong-doing, rebellion against God, and the inner state of our fallen nature – and Jesus died once for all those sins. If the world should last a thousand more years, or a thousand times a thousand, there will still only be one sacrifice for sin for ever. Eternity itself will require no more than the Son of God accomplished in his work on Calvary. He deserves to sit down!

In contrast, the Old Testament priests never sat down. They had to deal with a never-ending stream of sinners, sacrifices and blood, because the animal sacrifices couldn't take away sin (Hebrews 10:4). We could well ask why God ordained such ineffectual sacrifices. What was he trying to teach through this useless repetition? God wanted to make sure that we understand three things:

• *The helplessness of the sinner*. Doing good works can never deliver us from sin. We can't deal with the offences of the past by the good deeds of the future. Doing our best is not an option. We can't even achieve our best, let alone achieve anything adequate in God's sight. Sin can only be dealt with if God deals with it himself.

- *The seriousness of sin*. The animal sacrifices show that sin and death are inseparable. The lamb was killed, its life terminated, because of the filthiness of sin. It was the blood of the sacrifice that paid the penalty for sin. As Paul said, 'The wages of sin is death' (Romans 6:23).

- *The need for substitution*. The sinner brings the sacrifice, an animal without spot or blemish, to the altar. The beast is innocent, but by laying his hands on it, the individual transfers his sin, guilt and rebelliousness on to the animal, which then dies in his place. Jesus stands as the perfect substitute, and does what an animal never could: he dies for us willingly, consenting to be identified with sinners, and with understanding, freely undertaking to bear our sin.

Today give thanks that Christ is 'seated at the right hand of God' (Colossians 3:1). Sin has been dealt with, and his work is finished.

Day 29

Read Hebrews 10:11–18
Key verses: Hebrews 10:12–13

....

But when this priest had offered for all time one sacrifice for sins, he sat down at the right hand of God, [13]and since that time he waits for his enemies to be made his footstool.

The Lord Jesus is not only sitting (see Day 28), but also waiting – for his enemies to cave in, to surrender to his rule. Only one who has already achieved victory waits for the enemy to submit. It is folly to wait for submission if the battle has not yet been won. But Jesus has no more fighting to do. He is perfectly at rest at the right hand of God, simply waiting for the submission of his defeated foes.

Calvary was where Satan was defeated. On the cross the Lord was locked in single combat with the prince of this world. His disciples had abandoned him, and his Father turned his back on him, because he could not look on sin.

As darkness descended, and Jesus breathed his last, it looked as if hope had died. The disciples took his body down from the cross and buried it, until, on the third day, he rose throbbing with the life of God, radiant, glorious, from the tomb.

Satan's apparent victory was short-lived. The victory lay eternally with the Son of God because the Father heard his cry on the cross, 'It is finished!' We can imagine the Father's response – 'Is it? Is Satan really dealt with?' From Good Friday and all through the quietness and solemnity of the Saturday the Father was calculating, estimating whether our sin had truly been paid for. And on the third day, with the cry 'It is finished!' still ringing in his ears, the Father cried, 'Amen!', and raised his Son from the dead, evidence that the victory lies with the Christ of Calvary.

Do you know this victorious Lord Jesus in your life? Whatever temptations and trials Satan confronts you with, look upwards at Jesus on the throne and remember that no temptation can defeat him, and no trial unseat him.

Satan still prowls around like a roaring lion seeking to devour us (1 Peter 5:8). But don't lose heart. The Lord Jesus' decisive victory over Satan on the cross means that we can resist his attacks. The same power that raised Jesus from the dead is available to you. Today pray that you would treat Satan like the defeated enemy he is – don't give him room in your life, don't listen to his lies, don't give in to the temptations he puts before you, don't believe the doubt and despair he sows in your heart. Instead, pray for resurrection power to live the holy life Christ died to give you (Hebrews 10:14).

> I pray that the eyes of your heart may be enlightened in order that you may know . . . his incomparably great power for us who believe. That power is the same as the mighty strength he exerted when he raised Christ from the dead and seated him at his right hand in the heavenly realms.
> (Ephesians 1:18–20)

Day 30

Read 1 John 3:1–10
Key verses: 1 John 3:5–6

• •

But you know that he appeared so that he might take away our sins. And in him is no sin. ⁶No one who lives in him keeps on sinning. No one who continues to sin has either seen him or known him.

What is the bull's-eye of the gospel?

Jesus died to 'take away our sins' (verse 5). The cross of Christ is a picture of the horror of my sin and the length that a holy God had to go to to deal with it. He died to take the punishment we deserve for our rebellion against a holy God. He absorbed the righteous wrath of God against human sin.

John is telling us this not just so we get our theology about the cross right, but so that we will learn to hate sin in our own lives. He is unsettled by how easily Christians learn to live with the sin that nailed the Saviour to the cross. It is a complete contradiction, in John's mind, to call yourself a child of God, yet have a lax view of sin (verses 4–6). He says that when we sin, we actually live like children of the devil (verses 7–10).

John is not claiming, in verse 6, that we can be sinless in this life (1 John 1:8–10). He is saying that as Christians mature, they will – must – become more and more intolerant of sin in their lives. 'The reason the Son of God appeared was to destroy the devil's work' (verse 8), so how can we play with, tolerate, the very thing that Christ despises? The mark of the children of God is that they hate sin because they have fallen in love with Jesus.

Today come to the cross for the forgiveness and grace Christ offers. 'If anybody does sin, we have an advocate with the Father – Jesus Christ, the Righteous One. He is the atoning sacrifice for our sins, and not only for ours but also for the sins of the whole world' (1 John 2:1–2).

With God's strength, deal ruthlessly with the greed, lust, pride – whatever sin you have been complacent about – and strive for holiness. One day soon your transformation will be complete: 'When Christ appears, we shall be like him, for we shall see him as he is. All who have this hope in him purify themselves, just as he is pure' (1 John 3:2–3).

God wants you to be holy. Through faith, He already counts you holy in Christ. Now He intends to make you holy with Christ. This is no optional plan, no small potatoes. God saved you to sanctify you. God is in the beautification business, washing away spots and smoothing out wrinkles. He will have a blameless bride. He promised to work in you; He also calls you to work out. 'The beauty of holiness' is first of all the Lord's (Ps. 29:2, KJV). But by His grace it can also be yours.

(Kevin DeYoung, *The Hole in Our Holiness*, Crossway Books, 2012, p. 146)

For further study

If you would like to read more about the cross, you might find the following selection of books helpful:

- Don Carson, *Scandalous* (IVP, 2010).

- Tim Chester, *The Ordinary Hero* (IVP, 2009).

- Kevin DeYoung, Richard Coekin, Yannick Christos-Wahab, *The Cross in Four Words* (The Good Book Company, 2020).

- Tim Keller, *King's Cross* (Hodder and Stoughton, 2014).

- Mike McKinley, *Passion* (The Good Book Company, 2012).

- Jeremy and Elizabeth McQuoid, *The Amazing Cross* (IVP, 2012).

- Mark Meynell, *Cross-Examined* (IVP, 2021).

- Marcus Nodder, *Why Did Jesus Have to Die?* (The Good Book Company, 2014).

- John Stott, *The Cross of Christ* (IVP, 2006).

- Rankin Wilbourne and Brian Gregor, *The Cross Before Me: Reimagining the Way of the Good Life* (David C. Cook, 2019).

Keswick Ministries

Our purpose

Keswick Ministries exists to inspire and equip Christians to love and live for Christ in his world.

God's purpose is to bring his blessing to all the nations of the world (Genesis 12:3). That promise of blessing, which touches every aspect of human life, is ultimately fulfilled through the life, death, resurrection, ascension and future return of Christ. All of the people of God are called to participate in his missionary purposes, wherever he may place them. The central vision of Keswick Ministries is to see the people of God equipped, inspired and refreshed to fulfil that calling, directed and guided by God's Word in the power of his Spirit, for the glory of his Son.

Our priorities

There are three fundamental priorities which shape all that we do as we look to serve the local church.

- *Hearing God's Word*: The Scriptures are the foundation for the church's life, growth and mission, and Keswick Ministries is committed to preaching and teaching

God's Word in a way which is faithful to Scripture and relevant to Christians of all ages and backgrounds.

- *Becoming like God's Son*: From its earliest days, the Keswick movement has encouraged Christians to live godly lives in the power of the Spirit, to grow in Christ-likeness and to live under his Lordship in every area of life. This is God's will for his people in every culture and generation.

- *Serving God's mission*: The authentic response to God's Word is obedience to his mission, and the inevitable result of Christlikeness is sacrificial service. Keswick Ministries seeks to encourage committed discipleship in family life, work and society, and energetic engagement in the cause of world mission.

Our ministry

- *Keswick Convention*. The Convention attracts some 12,000 to 15,000 Christians from the UK and around the world to Keswick every summer. It provides Bible teaching for all ages, vibrant worship, a sense of unity across generations and denominations, and an inspirational call to serve Christ in the world. It caters for children of all ages and has a strong youth and young adult programme. And it all takes place in the beautiful

Lake District – a perfect setting for rest, recreation and refreshment.

- *Keswick fellowship*. For more than 140 years, the work of Keswick has affected churches worldwide, not just through individuals being changed, but also through Bible conventions that originate or draw their inspiration from the Keswick Convention. Today, there is a network of events that share Keswick Ministries' priorities across the UK and in many parts of Europe, Asia, North America, Australia, Africa and the Caribbean. Keswick Ministries is committed to strengthening the network in the UK and beyond, through prayer, news and co-operative activity.

- *Keswick teaching and training*. Keswick Ministries is developing a range of inspiring, equipping, Bible-centred teaching and training that focuses on 'whole-of-life' discipleship. This builds on the same concern that started the Convention, that all Christians live godly lives in the power of the Spirit in all spheres of life in God's world. Some of the events focus on equipping. They are smaller and more intensive. Others focus on inspiring. Some are for pastors, others for those in different forms of church leadership, while many are for any Christian. All courses aim to see participants return home refreshed to serve.

- *Keswick resources*. Keswick Ministries produces a range of books, devotionals and study guides as well as digital resources to inspire and equip Christians to live for Christ. The printed resources focus on the core foundations of Christian life and mission, and help Christians in their walk with Christ. The digital resources make teaching and sung worship from the Keswick Convention available in a variety of ways.

Our unity

The Keswick movement worldwide has adopted a key Pauline statement to describe its gospel inclusivity: 'All one in Christ Jesus' (Galatians 3:28). Keswick Ministries works with evangelicals from a wide variety of church backgrounds, on the understanding that they share a commitment to the essential truths of the Christian faith as set out in our statement of belief.

Our contact details

T: 017687 80075
E: info@keswickministries.org
W: www.keswickministries.org
Mail: Keswick Ministries, Rawnsley Centre, Main Street, Keswick, Cumbria CA12 5NP, England

Related titles from IVP

Food for the Journey

The Food for the Journey series offers daily devotionals from much loved
Bible teachers at the Keswick Convention in an ideal pocket-sized format –
to accompany you wherever you go.

Available in the series

1 Thessalonians

Alec Motyer with
Elizabeth McQuoid
978 1 78359 439 9

2 Timothy

Michael Baughen with
Elizabeth McQuoid
978 1 78359 438 2

Colossians

Steve Brady with
Elizabeth McQuoid
978 1 78359 722 2

Ezekiel

Liam Goligher with
Elizabeth McQuoid
978 1 78359 603 4

Habakkuk

Jonathan Lamb with
Elizabeth McQuoid
978 1 78359 652 2

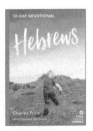

Hebrews

Charles Price with
Elizabeth McQuoid
978 1 78359 611 9

James

Stuart Briscoe with
Elizabeth McQuoid
978 1 78359 523 5

John 14 - 17

Simon Manchester with
Elizabeth McQuoid
978 1 78359 495 5

Available from your local Christian bookshop or **www.ivpbooks.com**

Food for the Journey

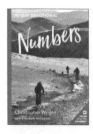   

Numbers
Christopher Wright
with Elizabeth
McQuoid
978 1 78359 720 8

Revelation 1 - 3
Paul Mallard with
Elizabeth McQuoid
978 1 78359 712 3

Romans 5 - 8
John Stott with
Elizabeth McQuoid
978 1 78359 718 5

Ruth
Alistair Begg with
Elizabeth McQuoid
978 1 78359 525 9

Praise for the series

'This devotional series is biblically rich,
theologically deep and full of wisdom . . .
I recommend it highly.' Becky Manley Pippert,
speaker, author of *Out of the Saltshaker and
into the World* and creator of the Live/Grow/
Know course and series of books

'These devotional guides are excellent tools.'
John Risbridger, Minister and Team Leader,
Above Bar Church, Southampton

'These bite-sized banquets . . . reveal our
loving Father weaving the loose and messy
ends of our everyday lives into his beautiful,
eternal purposes in Christ.' Derek Burnside,
Principal, Capernwray Bible School

'I would highly recommend this series of
30-day devotional books to anyone seeking
a tool that will help [him or her] to gain a
greater love of Scripture, or just simply . . .
to do something out of devotion. Whatever
your motivation, these little books are a must-
read.' Claud Jackson, *Youthwork* Magazine

Available from your local Christian bookshop or **www.ivpbooks.com**

Food for the Journey THEMES

The **Food for the Journey: Themes** offers daily devotions from much loved Bible teachers at the Keswick Convention, exploring how particular themes are woven through the Bible and what we can learn from them today. In a convenient, pocket-sized format, these little books are ideal to accompany you wherever you go.

Available in the series

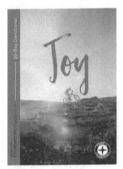

Joy
978 1 78974 163 6
'A rich feast!'
Edrie Mallard

Persevere
978 1 78974 102 5
'Full of essential theology.'
Catherine Campbell

Pray
978 1 78974 169 8
'The ideal reboot.'
Julian Hardyman

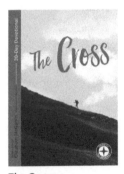

The Cross
978 1 78974 191 9
'A must-read.'
Gavin Calver

Confident
978 1 78974 190 2
'A beautiful collection.'
Elinor Magowan

Available from your local Christian bookshop or **www.ivpbooks.com**

Related teaching CD and DVD packs

CD PACKS

1 Thessalonians
SWP2203D (5-CD pack)

2 Timothy
SWP2202D (4-CD pack)

Colossians
SWP2318D (4-CD pack)

Ezekiel
SWP2263D (5-CD pack)

Habakkuk
SWP2299D (5-CD pack)

Hebrews
SWP2281D (5-CD pack)

James
SWP2239D (4-CD pack)

John 14 - 17
SWP2238D (5-CD pack)

Numbers
SWP2317D (5-CD pack)

Revelation
SWP2300D (5-CD pack)

Romans 5 - 8
SWP2316D (4-CD pack)

Ruth
SWP2280D (5-CD pack)

Available from www.essentialchristian.com

Related teaching CD and DVD packs

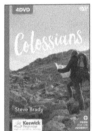

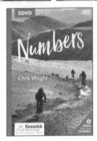
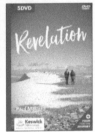

Colossians
SWP2318A (4-DVD pack)

Ezekiel
SWP2263A (5-DVD pack)

Habakkuk
SWP2299A (5-DVD pack)

John 14 - 17
SWP2238A (5-DVD pack)

Numbers
SWP2317A (5-DVD pack)

Revelation
SWP2300A (5-DVD pack)

Ruth
SWP2280A (5-DVD pack)